FEJ

GERMANY

WORLD ADVENTURES

BY EMMA CALWAY

©2017
Book Life
King's Lynn
Norfolk PE30 4LS

ISBN: 978-1-78637-140-9

Printed in Malaysia

Written by:
Emma Calway

Edited by:
Charlie Ogden

Designed by:
Matt Rumbelow

A catalogue record for this book
is available from the British Library.

GERMANY

WORLD ADVENTURES

CONTENTS

Page 4 Where is Germany?

Page 6 Weather and Landscape

Page 8 Clothing

Page 10 Religion and Festivals

Page 12 Food

Page 14 At School

Page 16 At Home

Page 18 Families

Page 20 Sport

Page 22 Fun Facts

Page 24 Glossary and Index

Words in **red** can be found in the glossary on page 24.

WHERE IS GERMANY?

Germany is a large country in Europe. It has nine countries around it, including France, Austria and Poland.

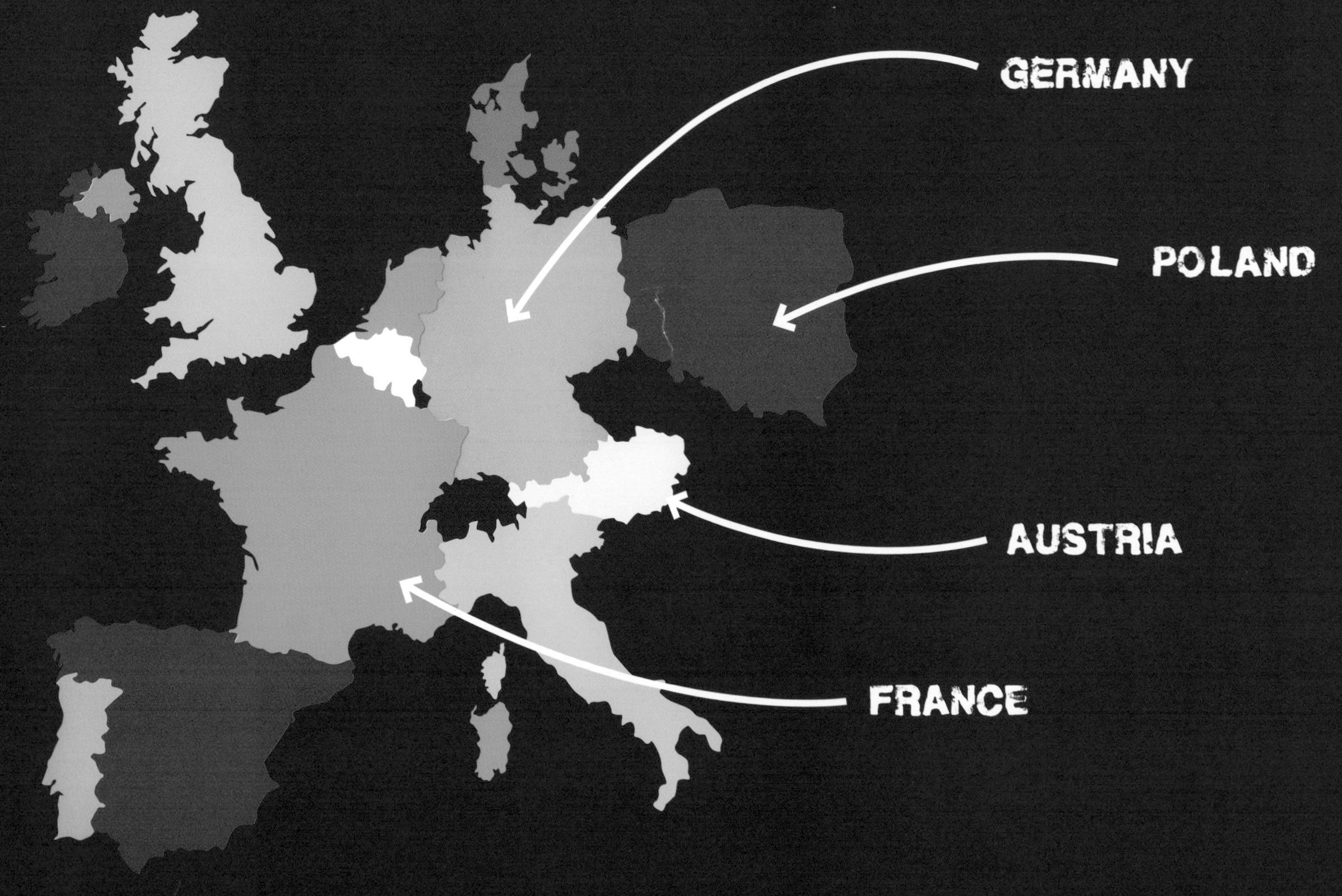

Over 80 million people live in Germany. The capital city of Germany is Berlin.

WEATHER AND LANDSCAPE

In summer it gets very hot. The hottest months are usually June, July and August. Germany often has cold winters with lots of snow.

Germany has many forests, rivers and mountains. The longest river is called the Rhine. In winter, people go on holiday there.

CLOTHING

Lederhosen are a type of **traditional** clothing worn by men in German. They come down to the knees and are worn with socks and shoes.

LEDERHOSEN

German women traditionally wore a long dress called a dirndl. Dirndls are worn with a white blouse and an apron.

RELIGION AND FESTIVALS

The **religion** with the most followers in Germany is Christianity. A Christian place of **worship** is a church.

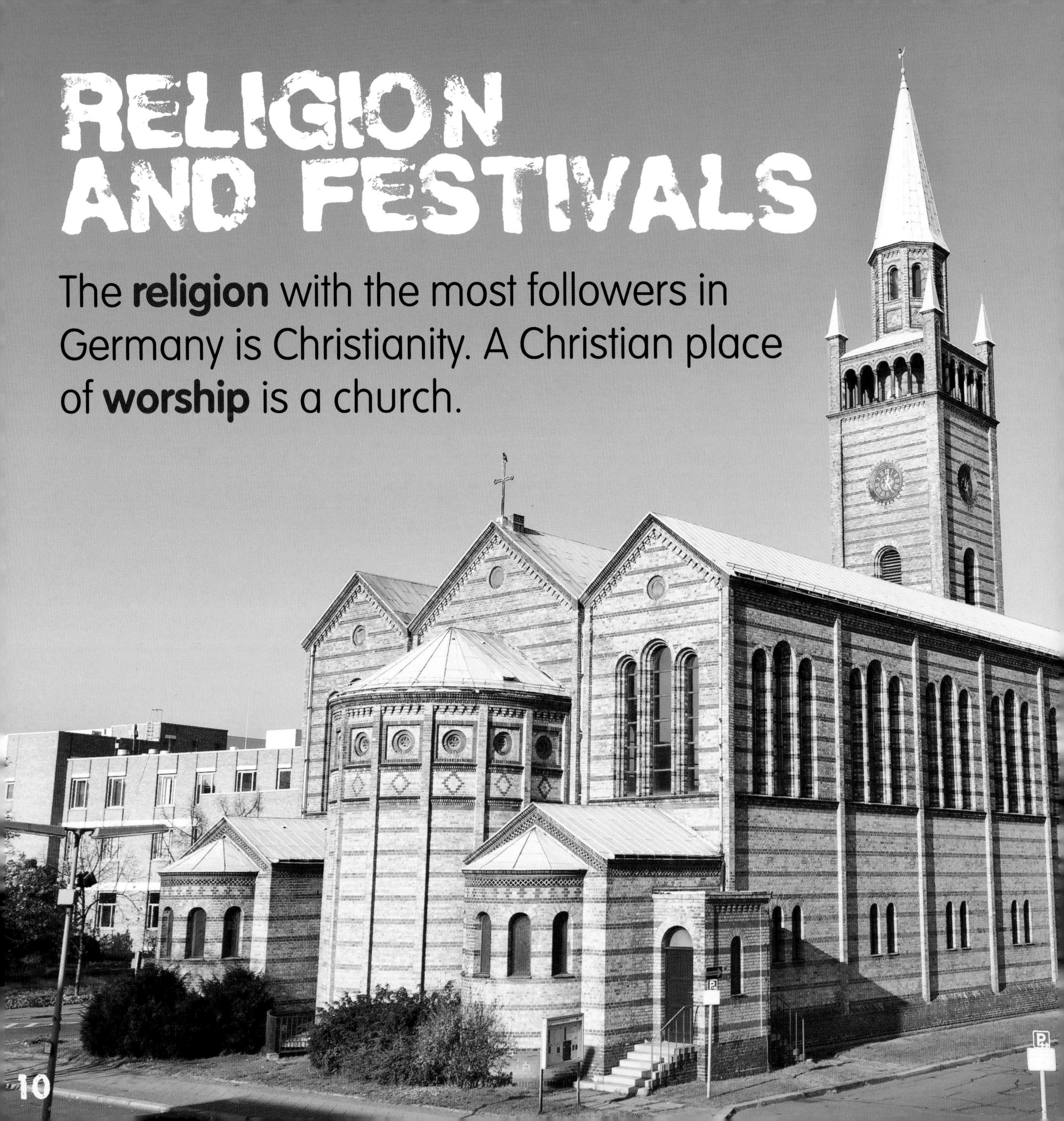

Oktoberfest is a **festival** that takes place in Germany every year. Men and women dress in lederhosen and dirndls and they often dance to music.

FOOD

Germans often eat meat as part of their main meal. Sauerbraten (sour roast) is one of the country's most popular dishes.

Germany is famous for its cakes. After lunch, people sometimes buy a slice of cake and a coffee.

AT SCHOOL

Children in Germany go to school from six years old. Many school children get to school by walking or by taking the bus.

Children learn many subjects at school including German, maths, science and languages. School often starts before 8 o'clock in the morning.

AT HOME

People in towns and cities in Germany usually live in tall blocks of flats. Around 3.5 million people live in Berlin.

In the villages there is more space. Many people live on farms and grow **crops**, such as wheat, barley and corn.

FAMILIES

Families in Germany are very like families in the rest of Europe. Children usually live at home with their parents and **siblings**.

German families usually get together to celebrate special **occasions**, such as birthdays and weddings. They usually celebrate with cake and presents.

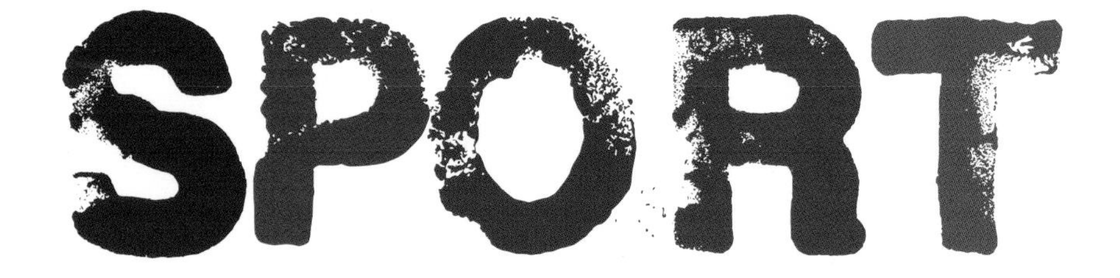

Tennis, motor racing and football are all popular sports in Germany.

Many Germans go to sport clubs to play sport. Other popular sports include handball, basketball and ice hockey.

The German football team has won four World Cups.

FUN FACTS

The tradition of putting fir trees in your home at Christmas started in Germany.

Germany's forests, the Black Forest and the Bavarian Forest, are home to wild boar, foxes and deer.

GLOSSARY

crops	plants grown by farmers to make food for people
festival	a celebration of a special event or time of the year
occasions	special events
religion	the belief in and worship of a god or gods
siblings	brothers and sisters
traditional	ways of behaving that have been done for a long time
worship	a religious act, such as praying

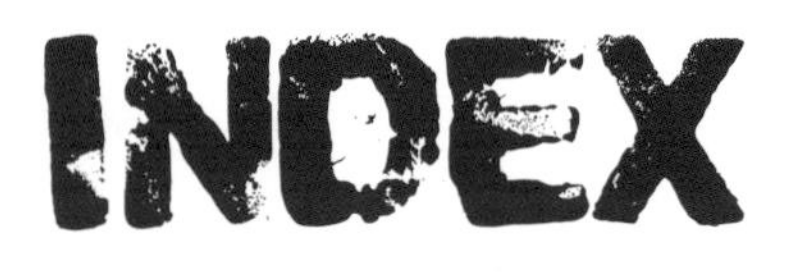

Berlin 5, 16
Christianity 10, 22
cities 5, 16
Europe 4, 18
food 12–13
football 20–21
forests 7, 23
schools 14–15
sports 20–21

Photocredits: Abbreviations: l-left, r-right, b-bottom, t-top, c-centre, m-middle.
Front Cover, Olga Sapegina, bg - Aleksey Klints,. 1 – Tiberiu Stan, 3 - Ramona Heim, 5 – canadastock, 6 - Andrew Mayovskyy, 7t – FamVeld, 7b – FamVeld, 8bl - Sharon Benton, 8 br - Markus Gann, 9 - Markus Gann, 10 - Anibal Trejo, 11 – tichr, 12 - TunedIn by Westend61, 13 - Zaretska Olga, 14 - Art Konovalov, 15 - Sergey Novikov, 16 - Tom Klimmeck, 17 – canadastock, 17tr - Ievgenii Meyer, 17rb - red mango, 17rm - Zeljko Radojko, 18 - Christin Lola, 19 - Boris Stroujko, 20 – holbox, 21 - Beto Chagas, 22 – TheBusinessMan, 23l – Robnroll, 23r - Neil Burton
Images are courtesy of Shutterstock.com, unless stated otherwise. With thanks to Getty Images, Thinkstock Photo and iStockphoto.